TIM TEBOW
Always a Hero

By Tim Polzer

SCHOLASTIC INC.

ISBN 978-0-545-48595-1

12 11 10 9 8 7 6 5 4 3 2 1   12 13 14 15 16/0

Printed in the U.S.A.   40
First printing, September 2012

TABLE OF CONTENTS

CHAPTER 1

TEBOWMANIA

On an unforgettable winter night, January 5, 2012, at Mile High Stadium in Denver, Colorado, Tim Tebow threw an amazing pass in the final seconds of a playoff game. This would be the defining moment in Tim Tebow's rise to stardom. Tebowmania was here to stay!

It was an 80-yard touchdown pass to Demaryius Thomas on the first play of overtime that gave the Denver Broncos a 29-23 upset win over the Pittsburgh Steelers in their AFC Wild Card Game.

As Thomas crossed the goal line, Tim got down on a knee and started to pray. His signature celebration—which had come to be known as "Tebowing"—had become popular with his growing number of fans in the NFL and athletes around the world.

Broncos fans were thankful that Tim had helped with another comeback win. Many fans and reporters had not believed Tim Tebow would be good enough to play quarterback in the NFL. They never would have thought he could be the leader in so many exciting victories, but Tim has been proving people wrong since the day he was born.

After a great college career that included two national championships at the University of Florida, many expected Tim to be a better runner than passer. He was bigger and more muscular than most NFL quarterbacks, and his throwing motion was unusual. Most thought he would never find the same level of success that he did in college. This did not discourage Tim, who only worked harder to prove he belonged in the NFL.

Tebowmania keeps growing thanks to Tim's ability to lead his team to huge wins. This is the story of how he overcame incredible odds to be one of the most inspiring players in all of sports.

CHAPTER 2

MEET THE TEBOWS

Tim Tebow was born outside the United States in the Philippines, a country in southeast Asia. Doctors were not sure if he would be a healthy baby. But he beat the odds and on August 14, 1987, little "Timmy" was born.

His parents, Bob and Pam, were American Baptist missionaries. They were working overseas to help needy people in the foreign country. The Tebows have always made their Christian beliefs and helping people a big part of their lives. Throughout Tim's childhood his family volunteered at missions, orphanages overseas, and charity programs in the United States.

As the youngest of five children, Tim and his family moved to a farm outside Jacksonville, Florida. He and his brothers and sisters were homeschooled by their mother, Pam, while Tim's father worked as a pastor. Unfortunately, being homeschooled meant not being able to play sports for a school team, but that was about to change.

CHAPTER 3

FROM HOMESCHOOL TO HIGH SCHOOL

Luckily for Tim (and football fans everywhere) a law was passed that allowed homeschooled students to play sports at the closest high school. Tim played linebacker and tight end at Trinity Christian Academy, but he really wanted to be a quarterback. In 2004, Tim and his mother moved to an apartment in Ponte Vedra, Florida, where he could play for Nease High School. The move was covered by media across the state and the nation. Tim Tebow was already in the national spotlight.

Tim was bigger than most high-school quarterbacks. His size allowed him to run and pass with great success. He also had a habit of playing through injuries. In one game, Tim felt a pain in his leg. He and his coaches thought he was just suffering from cramps. He told his coaches that he wanted to keep playing, and even ran for a touchdown in the second half. After the game, doctors discovered that he had played much of the game with a broken leg!

Tim quickly became one of the state's best high-school football players. He was named Florida's Player of the Year as a junior and led Nease to a state title as a senior. In three seasons at Nease, he passed for almost 10,000 yards and almost 100 touchdowns, and rushed for more than 3,000 yards and 63 touchdowns.

Tim's incredible high-school career continued as he was named Florida's Mr. Football and a PARADE magazine high-school All-American. He was selected to play on national television in the U.S. Army All-American Bowl and also was listed among the top 33 Florida high-school football players in the last 100 years.

Tim was rated as one of the nation's top quarterback recruits and his story was the subject of an ESPN television documentary. Many universities and colleges offered him football scholarships, including the University of Florida where his parents had gone to school. His mother and father wanted him to be happy wherever he decided to go, but his entire family was fans of the Gators. Tim chose Florida because coach Urban Meyer's offense was similar to how he played in high school. The next four years would prove that he made a great choice.

CHAPTER 4

COLLEGE CAREER

I t didn't take long for Tim Tebow to become an important part of the University of Florida's football team, even though he was not the starting quarterback. In his first game as a freshman in 2006, he even scored a touchdown.

Unlike most quarterbacks, Tebow was at his best near the goal line, leading the team with 8 rushing touchdowns. He finished the season ranked second on the team with 469 yards

rushing and was named to the All-SEC Freshman team. He also helped with the Gators' win over Ohio State in the BCS National Championship Game, passing and running for a touchdown.

During his sophomore year in the 2007 season, Tebow became the Gators' full-time starting quarterback. He was a double-threat to defenses, passing for 3,286 yards and 32 touchdowns while also rushing for 895 yards and 23 touchdowns. He became the only NCAA player to rush and pass for at least 20 touchdowns in a season.

At the end of the 2007 season, Tebow was awarded the Heisman Trophy as the nation's best college player. Tim Tebow made history as the first underclassman—a freshman or sophomore—to win the award.

Early in his junior season of 2008, Tebow showed great leadership again. Florida players and fans were very disappointed after the Gators lost to the University of Mississippi. Tebow saw a chance to lift up his team and school by apologizing to Florida fans:

"To the fans and everybody in Gator Nation, I'm sorry. I'm extremely sorry. We were hoping for an undefeated season. That was my goal, something Florida has never done here. I promise you one thing, a lot of good will come of this...."

Tebow's speech, which became known as "The Promise," came true. He helped the Gators win the rest of their games and beat top-ranked Oklahoma in the BCS National Championship Game. The school even put Tim's full speech on a plaque at Florida's Ben Hill Griffin Stadium.

After his senior season, Tebow was named a Heisman Trophy finalist for the third time. In four seasons, he had been honored with many awards. He was selected an All-American on the field

three times (2007, 2008, 2009) and an Academic All-American twice (2008 and 2009). He left Florida with two national championships and a degree in family, youth, and community sciences. The university would honor Tebow with a statue of him outside its stadium.

TIM TEBOW

CHAPTER 5

GOING PRO

Tim Tebow was a proven leader and winner in college, but most professional scouts did not think he could play in the NFL. His throwing motion needed to be perfected if he was going to be a great quarterback in the NFL.

Tim, who is left-handed, went to work at becoming a better passer. He wanted to prove that the people who didn't believe in him were wrong. Tim changed the way he held a football, holding it higher and near his shoulder, rather than closer to his waist. The change would allow him to throw the ball faster than before. He also practiced taking snaps from behind the center, rather than standing several yards back. He learned how to use his feet while dropping back to pass. Tebow's pre-Draft coaches were very impressed with how quickly he improved his game.

More than 100 NFL scouts and several thousand fans watched Tebow and other Florida players work out at the university before the Draft. Many fans of the Jacksonville Jaguars hoped the team would pick Tebow so he could play in his hometown. But there was still a lot of doubt about Tim's ability to play in the NFL. Would the quarterback who won two national titles and a Heisman Trophy be drafted at all?

The NFL Draft took place in New York City, but Tim decided to stay in Florida and watch it on television with his family and friends. Tim did not have to wait long. The Denver Broncos surprised many by trading up to select him in the first round with the twenty-fifth pick. Tebow was also happy that his extra work had paid off. He was ready for his life's next challenge: his rookie season in the NFL.

CHAPTER 6

ROOKIE SEASON

After the Draft, Denver Broncos head coach Josh McDaniels said Tim Tebow was tough and smart. Tim thanked McDaniels for believing in him, and set out to earn the team's trust. Tim began learning the Broncos' offense in training camp. It wasn't easy though because he was always being watched by reporters and TV cameras.

The Broncos thought Tebow had great promise, but they weren't ready to have him start for their team. They were preparing Tim to be their backup quarterback. This was not unusual for rookies although it had been a long time since Tim was in this position. He made the best of the situation, gaining as much experience in practice as he could. And Tim made sure not to get distracted by all of the attention.

While Tebow spent most of the season standing on the sideline as the team's third-string quarterback, he cheered on his teammates and learned how the more experienced quarterbacks play in the NFL.

Near the end of Tim's rookie season, the Bronco's starting quarterback, Kyle Orton, hurt his ribs. Coach McDaniels decided to let Tim start his first game. Tebow took over, passing for 308 yards. It was more than any rookie quarterback in Broncos history, including Hall of Fame quarterback John Elway. Tebow also threw a touchdown pass and ran for another to help the Broncos come back from a 17-0 deficit.

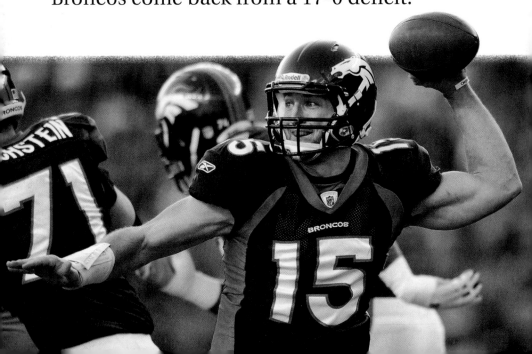

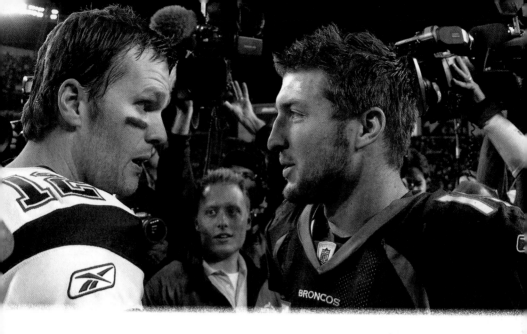

In the final three games of the 2010 season, Tebow rushed for 6 touchdowns, completed half of his passes, and threw 5 touchdowns. He finished the season with the best quarterback rating of all NFL rookies.

Broncos fans were very excited but Tebow had not yet convinced Denver's coaches that he should be the starting quarterback. He also had to gain the confidence of the Broncos' new vice president, John Elway. Despite the cheers of Broncos fans, Elway was not sure that Tebow had the talent to be the team's starting quarterback. Tim went into the offseason uncertain about his future.

CHAPTER 7

TEBOW TIME

At the start of his second season, Tim Tebow was back to being Denver Broncos' third-string quarterback. While many Broncos fans were disappointed, Tim continued to improve his skills. He helped the team any way he could, including playing wide receiver in one game. But Tim was a quarterback and wanted to lead Denver's offense.

He finally got a chance to show off in Week 5. The Broncos had been losing up to that point. Tim started at quarterback for the second half of the game and rallied Denver to two fourth-quarter scoring drives against the San Diego Chargers, including a 12-yard touchdown run and a 28-yard touchdown pass. The Broncos came up just short of an amazing comeback, but he was slowly gaining the confidence of his coaches and teammates.

In the next game against the Miami Dolphins, Tim set an NFL record by leading the Broncos to an overtime win on 2 touchdown drives and a two-point conversion—without any timeouts. The fifteen point fourth-quarter comeback was the largest in Broncos history. These late game comebacks began to be known as "Tebow Time."

With Tim starting at quarterback, the Broncos won six games in a row. Along the way Tim produced several unforgettable performances. He ran for a career-high 118 rushing yards and threw 2 touchdown passes against the Oakland Raiders. He also accounted for 92 of Denver's 95 yards in a game-winning drive against the New York Jets. He scored at least one rushing touchdown and a passing touchdown in seven games. He became the first quarterback in NFL history to lead 6 fourth-quarter comebacks in his first 11 games.

His shining moment of the breakout season was his first playoff start. Against Pittsburgh, Tim threw for more than 300 yards with just 10 completed passes against the NFL's best defense. He set up the Broncos' first 2 touchdowns with two 40-plus yard passes.

When the Steelers came from behind to tie the game in the fourth quarter, Tebow did not let his teammates get down. Instead, he opened overtime with the game-winning touchdown pass to Demaryius Thomas for the AFC Wild Card win. Tim was turning the people who doubted him into believers!

CHAPTER 8

THE TRADE

Tim had made a name for himself in Denver, but after the 2011 season, one of the top quarterbacks in the league became a free agent. Peyton Manning, a four-time MVP and former Super Bowl champion, was leaving the Indianapolis Colts. The Broncos couldn't pass up the opportunity to sign him. In March 2012, Peyton joined the team.

This was the end of Tebowmania in Denver. A few days later, Tim was traded to the New York Jets. Once again, Tim was faced with a challenge but he saw it as more of an opportunity. Tim held a press conference where he talked about being excited to join his new team.

Wherever Tim plays, there's sure to be a lot of excitement surrounding his game.

all things through hir

GRIFFIN STADIUM

TIM TEBOW
FOUNDATION

CHAPTER 9

HELPING OTHERS

With everything he has achieved, Tim Tebow learned at an early age that helping others was an important part of life. He and his family have worked hard for many years to help those who are less fortunate. He continues that practice today.

Tim helped raise money and supported charities while he played at the University of Florida. He has continued that mission as an NFL quarterback.

After being drafted by the Broncos, he started the Tim Tebow Foundation to aid the world's poorest children. One of the foundation's programs, Wish 15, helps grant the wishes of children with serious illnesses. In some cases, he has brought ailing children to Broncos games so he can meet and encourage them.

Tim also famously spent his entire signing bonus from the Broncos by donating it to charity. He gave away 2.5 million dollars in under 24 hours!

He has continued his parents' missionary work in the Philippines. His foundation is helping to build a children's hospital in that country, and he still spends time there.

Denver Mattress Co.®
Part of Furniture Row companies
Denver, Colorado

Date *July 21, 2011*

PAY TO THE
ORDER OF *Tim Tebow Foundation* $ **200,000**

Two Hundred Thousand DOLLARS

Tim enjoys talking about and working on his charity projects as much as he does preparing for his next NFL game. He celebrates his charity work and religion as much as he celebrates a touchdown. He hopes he can use his NFL success to help bring more faith, hope, and love into the lives of children everywhere.

Tim Tebow gives 100 percent of his heart and mind to whatever he is doing on or off the field.

CHAPTER 10

JUST THE FACTS

Full Name: Timothy Richard Tebow

Birthday: August 14, 1987

Hometown: Jacksonville, Florida

Parents: Bob and Pam Tebow

Siblings: Christy Allen, Katie Shepherd, Robby Tebow, Peter Tebow

High School Team: Nease Panthers (Allen D. Nease Senior High School, Ponte Vedra Beach, Florida)

College Team: Florida Gators (University of Florida, Gainesville, Florida)

Professional Team: New York Jets

Position: Quarterback

Jersey Number: 15

Throwing Hand: Left

Favorite Hobby: Studying NFL game film